Ella's kitchen

a tiny taste of the

First Foods Book

yummy recipes + top tips for
happy, healthy weaning

hamlyn

For the 130 million babies born
this year. Eat well, grow strong
– for this world is yours.

Paul + Alison Lindley

This special edition published in Great Britain
in 2015 by Hamlyn, a division of
Octopus Publishing Group Ltd,
Carmelite House,
50 Victoria Embankment,
London EC4Y 0DZ
www.octopusbooks.co.uk

An Hachette UK Company
www.hachette.co.uk

ISBN 9780600632825

A CIP catalogue record for this book is
available from the British Library

Typeset in Cooper Light and Ella's Kitchen®
Printed and bound in Italy

Created by Ella's Kitchen and Harris + Wilson

10 9 8 7 6 5 4 3 2 1

Recipe development: Nicola Graimes
Art direction, design + styling: Anita Mangan
Design assistant: Ella McLean
Photographer: Jonathan Cherry
Illustrations: Parker Williams Design
Managing editor: Judy Barratt
Assistant production manager: Lucy Carter
Home economist + food stylist: Lincoln Jefferson
Photoshoot direction: Sarah Ford, Caroline Harris +
Manisha Patel

Disclaimer Weaning should start when your baby is
around 6 months old. Children under the age of 6 months
with a family history of nut allergy, asthma, eczema or any
other type of allergy are advised to avoid eating dishes that
contain nuts. Check with a healthcare professional to make
sure you know which ingredients to avoid if you have a
child with allergies. Check all packaging for allergy advice
and use clean surfaces and utensils to avoid allergens
sneaking into your cooking. Never give whole nuts to
children under the age of 5 years in case of choking.
Some recipes contain honey. It is advised not to feed
honey to children under 12 months old. Every care should
be taken when cooking with and for children. Neither the
author nor the publisher can accept any liability for any
consequences arising from the use of this book, or the
information contained herein.

Publisher's notes
Standard level spoon measures are used in the recipes:

1 tablespoon = one 15 ml spoon
1 teaspoon = one 5 ml spoon
1 ice cube = one 15 ml spoon

Both metric and imperial measurements are given
for the recipes. Use one set of measurements only,
not a mixture of both.

Ovens should be preheated to the specified temperature.
For a fan-assisted oven, follow the manufacturer's
instructions to adjust the cooking time and temperature.

Medium-sized ingredients and pans and medium-strength
cheese have been used throughout unless otherwise
specified. Herbs are fresh unless otherwise specified.
Use low-salt stock, and avoid adding salt to recipes.

Freezing and storage
Freeze food in a freezer set at -18°C (0°F).
See pages 15 + 17 for further storage
and freezing information.

Contents

Foreword by Ella's dad

I look across the dinner table and see Ella, now 15 years old, talking about her day and I wonder where the years have gone. Fifteen years ago a high chair sat in that exact same spot, while a noisy toddler played loudly with her food; earlier still, it was the place of the first moments of her weaning journey.

Like any teenage girl, Ella can be selective about her culinary likes and dislikes, but she is always willing to try new things. Sometimes she discovers new tastes she loves (and sometimes she doesn't!). I like to think her willingness is the result of the ways in which we encouraged her to try new tastes and textures during the earliest moments, when *every* mouthful was an adventure.

Weaning can be one of the most enjoyable, but also the most frustrating and stressful times for both grown-ups and children. In the end only your instinct knows what works for you and your baby. The most important thing we've learned is that weaning is easiest when it's fun and messy and silly; when eating becomes an extension of play. I also believe that children are more likely to develop a lifelong love of food if they can build a relationship that puts food squarely into a social context – associating it with interactivity, eye contact, fun, enjoyment and being surrounded by the people they love.

Ella's weaning experience led directly to the seed of the idea that became Ella's Kitchen – that of aiming to provide healthy, handy and fun foods for children. This book joins you at the very beginning of your baby's foody journey. It puts you in charge, gives you choices, and through its tips and advice aims to help you develop the confidence to follow your instinct.

Keep smiling

Paul

Paul, Ella's dad

PS If your little one is hungry for more, the full version of *Ella's Kitchen The First Foods Book* is available to buy now.

Ella at the start of her weaning journey

Foreword by Vicky, Boots Parenting Club Nutrition Expert

Did you know that the word 'weaning' means to 'accustom'? It's certainly a learning experience for babies and new parents alike. Weaning is an important step in every baby's development because we now know that children's later food preferences are strongly influenced by their early eating experiences.

When the time is right, your baby will be eager to try new tastes and textures and hone his or her latest talents – grasping food with tiny hands, feeding from a spoon, learning to bite and chew and of course throwing food on the floor! It's the ideal time to establish healthy eating habits. However, when you are catering for first tastes a 'healthy' diet as we know it isn't ideal. Babies have tiny tummies so they need foods rich in calories and nutrients to help them grow. Low-fat or high-fibre foods will just fill them up too quickly, leaving little room for other nutritious foods. Weaning is also about training those tiny taste buds. You should avoid anything too sweet or too salty and aim to grow their taste repertoire to help to give them a healthy start in life.

While weaning time feels like a world away for me, I remember it fondly as messy and fun. My boys, Cameron and Jamie, are now strapping 10 and 13 year olds (and still messy!). I can't believe how keen they were to try my home-made creations and I'm proud of their adventurous tastes.

As a nutritionist, I felt confident about the what, when, why and how to wean but still had a lot to learn. You can never underestimate the value of real, hands-on experience.

Thank you to the Ella's Kitchen team for inviting me to share my first food thoughts and memories.

Enjoy every precious moment!

Vicky

Vicky Pennington,
Boots Parenting Club Nutrition Expert

Our first foods book

A bit about this book

You and your baby are about to embark on an amazing exploration of taste and texture, and we want to support you every step of the way. At Ella's Kitchen, our aim is to take the stress out of weaning so that you can create confident, happy mealtimes. We like to think of weaning as a journey of discovery for you and your baby – a sensory adventure that is packed with colour, and full of delicious, messy and noisy experiences.

Every baby is different and our book is all about helping you decide what's best for you and your family. We've given you lots of information and advice so that you can make informed choices about when and how to wean your baby, including how to read his or her own weaning signs. We've worked hard to develop recipes that will delight all your baby's senses and we hope that the extra tips, activities and games will make your baby's weaning journey a taste-tingling experience that starts with the very first mouthful.

Meet the experts

We've worked closely with a number of experts to make sure our recipes are as good for your baby as possible. Here are our recipe superstars:

Claire Baseley is an Infant Nutritionist. She's helped us make sure all our ingredients are really good for tiny tummies and growing bodies.

Nicola Graimes is an award-winning cookery author, specializing in children's nutrition. She's helped us write all the book's delicious recipes.

Dr Carmel Houston-Price is a Developmental Psychologist who works with us to understand the role of the five senses in the way a baby develops healthy attitudes towards food.

Sally Luckraft is our Food Developer. She makes all Ella's yummy new stuff. She's helped make sure our recipes will tingle little taste buds.

Top tips from our friends

We asked lots of Ella's Friends for their best weaning advice. Here are their top four nuggets of wisdom:

Go at your own pace It's so easy to compare your baby to all the others you know, but every baby is different and will be ready for new experiences at different times. Let *your* little one set the pace.

Love the mess Messy little faces and sticky little hands are inevitable – and they are the best signs of a fun mealtime.

The more the merrier Parents, grandparents and siblings – let everyone take a turn helping during this exciting time in your baby's life; your baby will love it!

Be kind to your time Plan your meals, shop online or locally, and learn recipe cheats – that way you'll have extra time to really enjoy the weaning experience with your baby.

Key to icons

At the top of every recipe, you'll find a combination of the following symbols to help make the job of weaning your baby as easy as it can be.

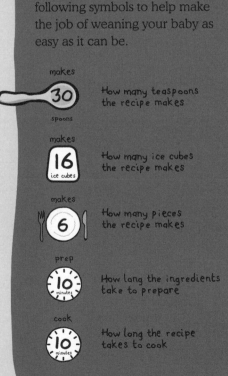

makes
30
spoons
How many teaspoons the recipe makes

makes
16
ice cubes
How many ice cubes the recipe makes

makes
6
How many pieces the recipe makes

prep
10 minutes
How long the ingredients take to prepare

cook
10 minutes
How long the recipe takes to cook

How to start your baby's weaning journey

What is weaning?

Weaning is the exciting time when babies stop being wholly reliant on breastmilk or formula and begin their foody adventures.

Knowing when to begin

Advice about when to begin weaning varies all over the world. Some countries, such as the UK and USA, advise introducing solids at around 6 months old, when a baby's digestive system is usually developed enough to cope with foods other than milk. Other countries, however, suggest beginning as early as 17 weeks (4 months) old.

Everyone agrees that before 17 weeks is too young. Not only is your baby's tummy not ready then, his or her kidneys aren't yet strong enough to cope with an increased workload.

Every baby is unique, so it's impossible to be prescriptive about *the* right time for babies in general. That's why it's really important you look for the signs your own baby gives you that he or she might be gearing up for some solids – we've put those signs in the yellow box, opposite, as a handy reference.

Then, if your baby is ready, but is younger than 6 months old, there are certain foods you should avoid giving, as they may cause allergies or make your baby poorly. We've listed these for you on page 21. Check with your health visitor if you have any questions or concerns.

It's all about taste

At 6 months old weaning is more about taste than it is about nutrition – your baby is still getting essential nutrients from breastmilk or formula. With taste in mind, the more variety babies try, the more likely they are to become good little eaters later on.

Of course, your baby might not like every new taste you present. Don't give up! You may need to offer a new taste on up to 10 separate occasions – or more – before your little one learns to love what you're giving. Keep trying, but don't force the issue. Try to make weaning a relaxed and happy time.

Some parents worry their baby isn't getting enough food in the early weeks of weaning. Try to relax. Your baby's tummy really is still tiny and milk continues to be *the* primary source of nutrition for a good while yet. As long as your baby is drinking milk, and you and your health visitor are happy your baby is growing well, you're doing fine.

Your baby's weaning signs

There are some common myths about when babies are ready to wean. For example, chewing fists, reaching for other people's food, waking in the night and wanting more milk can just be signals that your baby is doing all the normal things that babies do. They may not mean that your baby is ready for solid food at all. Babies are probably ready to start weaning when they can:

☺ Hold their head straight up on their own, and sit confidently with support.

☺ Show good hand–eye coordination, getting all their favourite toys – among other things – into their mouths.

Trust your instinct and you'll know when the time is right. Then, if when you start your baby just pushes out what you give, don't worry – wait a week or two and try again.

Foods to avoid

When you begin the weaning journey, not every food is good for your baby's tiny tummy. As well as the common allergens (see p.21), the following are foods you need to be extra-specially careful about.

Added salt Little ones under a year old need less than 1 g of salt – or 0.4 g of sodium – a day, so added salt is a no-no. Look out! Processed foods not intended for babies, such as pasta sauces, breakfast cereals and crisps, could have added salt in them; and stock cubes, too.

Added sugar Your baby is sweet enough, so avoid adding sugar in your cooking. Natural sugars in fruits provide plenty of sweetness – any more could lead to tooth decay or an unhealthy sweet tooth.

Honey Bears may like honey, but little ones shouldn't try it until they reach 1 year old, as it contains bacteria that could be harmful to tiny tummies.

Whole nuts Whole nuts, including peanuts, are easy to choke on. Don't give them until your child is over 5 years old.

Low-fat foods Low-fat yogurt, fromage frais, cheese or spreads are not 'baby's choice'. Babies need fat – it's a *reeeally* important source of calories and vitamins. You may be able to introduce low-fat foods after your little one's second birthday, but check with your doctor first.

Some fish + shellfish Some fish, including shark, marlin and swordfish, can contain high levels of mercury. Avoid giving these for the first year and after that only in small amounts. Oily fish can contain pollutants so limit to twice a week. Shellfish can carry a risk of food poisoning if it's undercooked.

Eggs Until your baby is 1 year old, give well-cooked eggs only – there is a tiny chance of salmonella in runny eggs.

Unpasteurized + blue cheeses Soft, unpasteurized cheeses, such as Brie and Camembert, and 'mouldy' or 'blue' cheeses, such as Stilton, carry a small risk of food poisoning and are best saved for after your baby's all-important first birthday.

Your baby's milk

Up until the age of 6 months, little ones get all the nutrients they need from breastmilk or formula milk. After 6 months, solid food starts to play a more important role in growth and development and your baby's daily milk intake will start to plateau. Between 6 months and a year, babies still need around 500–600 ml (17 fl oz–1 pint) of breastmilk or formula each day.

You can use cow's milk in cooking once your baby reaches 6 months old, but don't introduce cow's milk as a drink until after a year (see p.21), and then only if it is full fat. You may be able to introduce semi-skimmed milk from 2 years old.

Nutritionist know-how

'If, at 6 months old, your baby goes off milk when you start on food, don't panic! Use the baby's usual milk in your cooking, too – add it to rice pudding, macaroni cheese or custard to pack in those essential nutrients.'

Introducing other drinks

At the start of weaning, breastfed babies can reach their fluid requirements from milk alone (formula-fed babies may need a top-up of cooled, once-boiled water in hot weather). From 6 months, *as well as* your baby's usual milk, you can introduce water from a mains tap, in a baby cup or beaker. (Never use mineral water, as it can have high salt levels.) You can also give unconcentrated, pure fruit juice diluted 1 part juice to 10 parts water (brush tiny teeth regularly, though) at mealtimes. Always avoid squash and cordial, as they contain high amounts of processed sugar.

Good little eaters

We want your little one to develop a lifelong positive relationship with food. Here are a few ways to set your baby off on the right track.

Starting with savoury

Starting weaning with green and white veg can help little ones get used to more bitter flavours early on. We've given you step-by-step guidance on one way to approach a savoury first 2 weeks on pages 22-23.

Variety, variety, variety

Offering a variety of appropriate foods and textures is super-important. A rainbow of colours (see right), different sources of proteins, carbohydrates and fats, and different herbs and spices will encourage your baby to accept new foods as he or she grows up, even into adulthood. Try to offer your baby different tastes every day.

Baby knows best

Most babies know when they've had enough to eat. Follow your baby's lead. To tell you that enough is enough, babies might turn away their head, spit out their food, or push away the bowl or spoon.

Taking a turn

As soon as possible, put a spoon in your baby's little hand to have a go – it's a great way to learn the ropes!

Happy about food

Here are some more ideas on ways to make your baby's mealtimes fun:

☺ **It's a rainbow** Presenting lots of colourful foods makes dishes look more appealing – and lots of colours indicate all-round nutritional content.

☺ **Story time** Make up stories and songs involving broccoli trees, cauliflower sheep, strawberry hedgehogs…

☺ **Pick me up** Give whole or chopped-up veg and fruit to your little one to hold – little fingers love to explore the textures. And encourage messy play with food, which can help babies develop a positive foody relationship.

☺ **Family experiences** Eat together whenever you can, showing that mealtimes are sociable occasions.

Good in every sense

Our research has shown us that little ones who are able to experience veggies and fruit using all their senses are much more likely to eat those foods when mealtimes come around and to have a lifelong positive relationship with food. That's why we've put lots of ideas throughout the book for sensorial games you can try together. Let's play!

Feed the senses

Our friends say...

'Playing music is a great way to help both you and your little one relax and have fun at mealtimes. My baby and I love singing along to foody songs.'

Tongue-ticklingly tasty...

Babies have three times more taste buds than grown-ups, so trying new foods is really exciting for them. Our recipes use lots of herbs and spices and exciting ingredients to get tongues zinging!

Smells super...

Our sense of smell is essential to our sense of taste. Encourage your baby to smell food before eating it to get the full flavour experience. Mmmmm...

Touchy feely...

As little ones grow up, they recognize different foods by texture. Being able to hold ingredients and finger foods is important for this developmental step.

Looks lovely...

When discovering food, colour and shape are really important – offer a rainbow of foods in different shapes and sizes.

Sounds scrummy...

Foods make all sorts of sounds: carrots snap, onions sizzle, sauces bubble... Listen to the sounds of cooking and eating together, and make lots of 'yumminess' sounds during mealtimes. (Download some 'Tasty Tunes' from our website, too!)

Store-cupboard superheroes

Juggling a baby and everyday life is hard work! Even the most organized wonder-mums and super-dads can get caught short.

We believe that with a few store-cupboard essentials tucked away in the kitchen, anyone can whip up a delicious, nutritious meal for a little one in no time at all.

Pasta, rice + couscous

These are perfect accompaniments, but also delicious stirred through a sauce (see below).

Canned tomatoes + tomato purée

Add a few herbs and there's your sauce!

Canned pulses

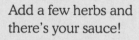

Butter beans and lentils provide texture and flavour, and are fantastic sources of protein.

Canned fish

Sardines and salmon can provide instant sources of protein and healthy fats.

Rolled oats

These are brilliant for simple breakfasts, or mixed with fruit for a pudding.

Dried herbs + spices

Cinnamon, oregano, thyme and turmeric can transform simple dishes.

Dried fruit

Raisins, sultanas and dark, unsulphured apricots make perfect toddler finger foods; or whiz them with some yogurt for an instant pudding.

Eggs

A mashed-up boiled egg or well-cooked scramble provides instant nutrition. Mixed with flour and some milk, eggs make a batter for pancakes, too.

Frozen veg

Veggies that are always fresh! A bag of frozen peas or broccoli means that supergreen nutrition is always at hand.

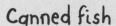

Safe + secure

Following a few simple rules helps keep little ones as safe as possible on their weaning adventure.

Wipe clean

Keep surfaces, chopping boards and utensils spotlessly clean. Use separate chopping boards for meat and veg.

Clean hands

Always wash your own hands before preparing any food. Then, check that your baby's hands are clean before eating. It's never too early to get babies into the habit of hand-washing before a meal.

Wash, peel + scrape

Wash all ingredients and either peel or scrub away tough skins before you cook.

Clean bowls + spoons

If your baby is younger than 6 months, sterilize all your feeding equipment (see p.16). After that, just make sure everything is washed really well in hot, soapy water and rinsed in clean water.

Hot, hot, hot

Cook or reheat food so it's piping hot all the way through, then stir it and cool it to a lukewarm temperature. Test it against your bottom lip to make sure it's just right for your baby. Never reheat cooked food more than once, and never refreeze food that's been frozen and then defrosted.

Two's company

Never leave your baby alone when eating or drinking – you need to be around in case of any mishaps, including choking.

Be cool

If you want to refrigerate (or freeze) food, make sure it's completely cold first. Cool it quickly – within 2 hours of cooking – by standing the container of food in a bowl of cold water. Once it's thoroughly cold, pop it in the fridge (or freezer).

Store safely

Keep cooked and raw meats covered and away from each other. Place cooked foods above raw foods in the fridge, and put non-meat foods on a separate fridge shelf.

Keep it fresh

Here are some guidelines for storing freshly made foods:

 In the fridge: 2 days in an airtight container

 In the freezer: up to 1 month at -18°C/0°F

 Cakes + bakes: in the cupboard for up to 3–4 days in an airtight container

Your weaning kitchen

What you'll need

So, before you get started, here's our guide to a few essentials you'll need in your kitchen to make it easier to prepare and store your baby's food.

- ☺ **Vegetable peeler** because you'll be doing a *lot* of peeling

- ☺ **Sharp paring knife** to chop things up nice and small

- ☺ **Small saucepans** that are perfect sizes for reheating little portions

- ☺ **Steamer**… but that needs a section all of its own (see opposite)

- ☺ **Sieve** to strain fruit, catch naughty pips and help get rid of tough skins

- ☺ **Hand blender** or **food processor** to whiz your baby's food to the right texture (food processors are better for tougher skins on veggies)

- ☺ **Potato masher** for when your little one moves on from purée

- ☺ **Sterilizer** for spoons and bowls, but only if you're weaning before your baby is 6 months old (you can sterilize in boiling water if you prefer)

- ☺ **Ice-cube trays** for storing purées in the freezer in portions

- ☺ **Freezer bags** for storing frozen purée cubes, or for freezing finger foods

- ☺ **Labels + marker pen** so you know what's what and when you made it

- ☺ **Beakers + cups** to help your baby move on from a bottle

- ☺ **Plastic spoons + bowls** for feeding time itself

- ☺ **High chair** or **booster seat** so your little one can sit at the table

- ☺ **Bibs** – we like the plastic ones with a tray to catch the bits

- ☺ **Face cloths** or **muslins** for wiping messy hands and faces

Getting steamy!

Steaming food is the best way to preserve nutrients and keep flavour locked in. Steam veggies until just tender – they're less tasty when they're mushy. Here are some steaming methods to choose from.

Dedicated steamer Some steamers are fancy electrical tiered units, while others look like a stack of saucepans with holes in.

Steamer basket These are holey baskets with little feet – they look like little spaceships. You put them in a saucepan with a little boiling water, cover and steam away.

Colander Pop your colander in a pan with a little water and cover it with a lid – hey presto, the steamer you never knew you had!

Microwave Put a little water in a microwave bowl, add the veggies and cover with clingfilm. Pierce the film and then zap in the microwave until the veggies are tender (about 2–3 minutes for leafy greens and 5–6 minutes for chopped root veg – but check your user guide).

Our friends say...

'Once my baby had moved on from single purées, I loved mixing and matching my ice cubes (see below) into interesting flavour combinations!'

Freezer essentials

Freezing your baby's food in batches can help make weaning *soooo* much easier, especially in the early stages. The quantities of our purée recipes for 6 and 7 months are given in ice cubes (1 ice cube = about 3 teaspoons). A guide to portion size is given at the start of each chapter to help you decide how much to defrost.

☺ Make sure your purées are completely cooled (see p.15) before you put them in the freezer.

☺ Label freezer bags with the name of the food and the date you made it.

☺ Use frozen food within 1 month.

☺ Defrost your food completely before reheating it. The safest ways to defrost are covered in the fridge overnight, or in a microwave.

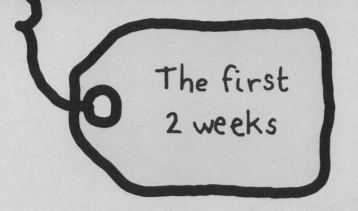

The first 2 weeks

Your baby is ready and it's time to get started. Here is the essential information you need to make sure you both put your best weaning feet forward.

Best first foods

New research tells us that offering only veggies for the first 2 weeks of weaning is a great way to entice tiny taste buds to love a whole range of flavours. In fact, babies weaned this way ate more veggies when aged 12 months compared to those who ate only fruits. The table on the following page is our step-by-step guide to this 'veg first' approach. Don't be surprised if your baby screws up that little face at first – breastmilk is sweet, so savoury flavours may be a bit of a surprise. Go gently, offer the same taste often, so little ones learn to love new foods and don't worry if your baby seems to eat very little – remember, it's all about taste for now.

If your baby isn't 6 months old yet, there are some foods that you need to avoid because they increase the risk of little ones developing allergies. Take a look at our box (opposite) for a handy guide, and consult your doctor if you're unsure.

Tips on texture

Although they can't chew yet, babies can move food from the front to the back of their mouths, and swallow.

We often call very first foods 'solids', but there's really very little that's solid about them just yet! Try to create the texture of double cream or runny honey (like in the picture, above) in a perfectly smooth purée. You'll probably need to loosen the consistency of the puréed food with a little boiled water, or with a little of your baby's usual milk, if you prefer.

Perfect timing

A new flavour once a day is just right for the first 2 weeks. Pick a time to start when your baby isn't too hungry – usually just after or during a milk feed – and not too tired. Leave plenty of time to enjoy the experience – don't start weaning when you've planned a busy day.

How much?

At the start of weaning, babies still get their nutrition from their usual milk – around 500–600 ml (17 fl oz–1 pint) a day – so try not to worry about how much solid food goes in. Right now, it's all about the flavour variety (and getting used to a spoon). Defrost just 1 ice cube at a time (see p.17 for how to do this safely), because a weaning spoonful or two is often plenty at the start. Take your baby's lead (see p.12).

Allergy essentials

Before 6 months of age, babies' digestive systems are very sensitive to the effects of certain 'allergen' foods. Even after 6 months, if you have a family history of allergies such as eczema or asthma, or of any food allergy, check with your doctor before you offer any of the following.

Allergen foods to avoid

☹ Wheat, gluten, nuts + seeds

☹ Eggs

☹ Fish + shellfish

☹ Nuts (including peanuts)

☹ Soybeans

☹ Celery + celeriac

☹ Cow's milk + other dairy products

☹ Mustard

☹ Sesame

Signs of an allergic reaction

Always keep an eye out for potential allergic reactions. Signs to watch for are:

☹ Irritated skin or a red rash, especially on your baby's face

☹ Swollen lips + mouth

☹ Runny nose + watery eyes

☹ Tummy upsets, including pain, vomiting or very runny poo

☹ Difficulty breathing (extreme cases)

If you're at all worried, consult your doctor or health visitor; and if your baby shows any signs of breathing difficulties, go straight to hospital.

Our first tastes weaning planner

We know those very first steps on your baby's weaning journey can feel a bit daunting. To help you, we've created this 2-week weaning planner. It uses a 'veg first' weaning approach (see p.12) to help get your baby used to savoury rather than sweet tastes as early as possible. Stay focused on building your little one's positive relationship with food – follow your instinct, listen to your baby, and most of all have *lots* of messy fun.

	Day 1	Day 2	Day 3	Day 4	Day 5	Day 6	Day 7
Week 1	potatoes	broccoli	cauliflower	green beans	cabbages	avocado	peas
Week 2	courgettes	Brussels sprouts	aubergine	carrots	parsnips	butternut squash	swede

1–2 spoonfuls just after lunchtime milk*

* Or, whatever time suits you and your baby best!

Using the planner

The planner suggests *one new veggie taste once a day, every day,* for the first 2 weeks. All the recipes for these purées are on pages 24–7.

We think just after a lunchtime milk feed is a good time to start your baby's very first tastes – but work with what suits you and your baby best. And remember that tiny amounts – just one or two weaning spoonfuls at a time – are probably enough.

Keep up the milk

As the first steps in weaning are just about taste, it's really important that babies keep to their usual routine and amounts (see p.21) when it comes to milk feeds – they still need all the goodness in breastmilk or formula to keep them healthy.

You can substitute your baby's usual milk for the water in the recipe when you need to thin a purée, if you prefer.

After the first 2 weeks

Keep offering veg or fruit (see below) one at a time and, when you feel ready, move on to simple combinations. Once babies are over 6 months of age and ready for more exciting combos, they can try all the yummy recipes in the following chapter.

Our friends say...

'I wanted my baby to associate her high chair with having lots of fun, so in the week before we started weaning, I'd sit her in it to play games and sing songs. Then, when the food came, she knew that was going to be fun, too!'

Other favourite very first foods

We think variety is so important for your baby. Below are some other favourite first tastes he or she might like. All of these fruits and veggies need to be peeled, and all but banana will need to be cooked until tender so that you can whiz the flesh into a super-soft purée (adding a little of your baby's usual milk if you need to). For banana, mash until smooth with the back of a fork and mix it with a little breastmilk or formula so that it's not too sticky.

 cucumber   sweet potatoes   pumpkin   apples   bananas   mangoes   pears   peaches   plums

23

Potatoes

makes **20** spoons

cook **20** minutes

1 **potato** (about 200 g/7½ oz), such as Maris Piper, peeled and cut into 1 cm/½ inch cubes

Cook the potato in a small saucepan of boiling water for 20 minutes until very tender, then drain, reserving the cooking water. Transfer the potato to a bowl and gradually add 60 ml/ 2½ fl oz of the reserved cooking water, mashing with a fork between each addition until the purée is loose enough that a little on the end of a spoon falls off sideways without any shaking.

Broccoli

makes **20** spoons

cook **10** minutes

½ small head **broccoli** (about 130 g/ 4½ oz), cut into small florets

Steam or boil the broccoli in a saucepan over a medium heat for 8 minutes until very tender. Adding 2–3 tablespoons boiled water, purée the broccoli in a food processor, or using a hand blender, until smooth.

You can thin all the purées using your baby's usual milk, if you prefer!

Cauliflower

makes **30** spoons

cook **10** minutes

⅓ small head **cauliflower** (about 140 g/5 oz), cut into small florets

Steam or boil the cauliflower in a saucepan over a medium heat for 8–10 minutes until very tender. Adding 4–5 tablespoons boiled water, purée the cauliflower in a food processor, or using a hand blender, until smooth.

Green beans

makes **20** spoons

cook **10** minutes

100 g/3½ oz **green beans**, trimmed and halved

Steam or boil the beans in a saucepan over a medium heat for about 7 minutes until very tender. Gradually adding 3–4 tablespoons boiled water, purée the beans in a food processor, or using a hand blender, until smooth. Pass the purée through a sieve to remove any fibrous pieces before serving.

Cabbages

makes **15** spoons

cook **5** minutes

¼ **white cabbage** (about 130 g/4½ oz), cored and finely chopped

Steam or boil the cabbage in a saucepan over a medium heat for about 5 minutes until very tender. Adding 2–3 tablespoons boiled water, purée the cabbage in a food processor, or using a hand blender, until smooth. Pass the purée through a sieve to remove any fibrous pieces before serving.

Avocado

serves **1**

cook **no cook**

1 very ripe **avocado**, peeled, stoned and chopped

Baby's usual milk (optional)

Using the back of a fork, mash the avocado until completely smooth, adding a little of your baby's usual milk if necessary. Alternatively, purée using a hand blender. (Mashed avocado won't keep, so discard any leftovers.)

Peas

makes **30** spoons

cook **15** minutes

150 g/5½ oz **frozen peas**

Steam or boil the peas in a saucepan over a medium heat for 10–12 minutes until completely tender. Purée the peas with 3–4 tablespoons of boiled water in a food processor, or using a hand blender, until completely smooth. Pass the purée through a sieve to remove any pieces of skin, if necessary.

Courgettes

makes **20** spoons   cook **10** minutes

1 **courgette** (about 150 g/5½ oz),
    halved lengthways and cut into
    5 mm/¼ inch thick slices

Steam or boil the courgette in a
saucepan over a medium heat
for 8–10 minutes until completely
tender. Purée in a food processor,
or using a hand blender, until smooth.

Brussels sprouts

makes **30** spoons   cook **15** minutes

150 g/5½ oz **Brussels sprouts**

Cut off the base of the sprouts and
remove the outer leaves. Cut the sprouts
in halves or quarters and steam over a
medium heat for about 10–12 minutes
until very tender (steaming is best as
boiled sprouts can taste bitter). Purée
the sprouts with 4–5 tablespoons of
boiled water in a food processor, or
using a hand blender, until smooth.

Stronger
flavours add to
your baby's foody
adventure.

Aubergine

makes **35** spoons   cook **10** minutes

1 **aubergine** (about 250 g/9 oz),
    cut into 1 cm/½ inch cubes

Steam the aubergine over a medium
heat for 10 minutes until the skin and
flesh are completely tender. Purée
the aubergine with 2–3 tablespoons
of boiled water in a food processor,
or using a hand blender, until smooth.
Pass the purée through a sieve to
remove any pieces of skin, if necessary.

Carrots

makes **30** spoons   cook **15** minutes

3 **carrots** (about 250 g/9 oz), peeled
    and halved lengthways

Slice the carrots into half-moon
shapes, 5 mm/¼ in thick. Steam or
boil the carrots in a saucepan over a
medium heat for 10–12 minutes until
completely tender. Purée the carrots
with 3–4 tablespoons of boiled water
in a food processor, or using a hand
blender, until completely smooth.

Parsnips

makes **30** spoons   cook **15** minutes

2 **parsnips** (about 350g/12 oz), peeled and cut into 1 cm/½ inch cubes

Steam or boil the parsnips in a saucepan over a medium heat for 10–12 minutes until very tender. Purée the parsnips with 150–175 ml/5–6 fl oz boiled water in a food processor, or using a hand blender, until smooth.

Butternut squash

makes **30** spoons   cook **15** minutes

½ **butternut squash** (about 250 g/9 oz), peeled

Cut the squash in half and scoop out the seeds. Cut the flesh into 1 cm/ ½ inch cubes. Steam or boil the squash in a saucepan over a medium heat for 15 minutes, or until very tender. Purée the squash with 4–5 tablespoons of boiled water in a food processor, or using a hand blender, until smooth.

Swede

makes **30** spoons   cook **20** minutes

½ **swede** (about 250 g/9 oz), peeled and cut into 1 cm/½ inch cubes

Steam or boil the swede cubes in a saucepan over a medium heat for about 20 minutes until completely tender. Purée the swede with 4–5 tablespoons of boiled water in a food processor, or using a hand blender, until smooth.

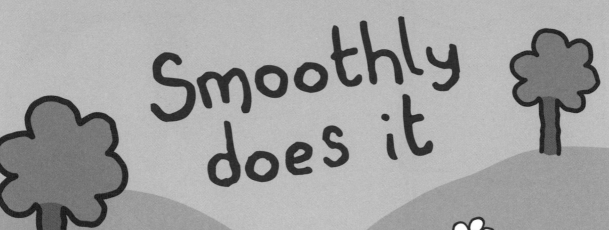

Smoothly does it

Now you're 6 months old you can try some new and exciting taste combinations! Come on, what are you waiting for?

From 6 months

Now that your little one has started to learn about the world of food and how individual flavours taste, you can begin to combine different flavours and introduce new food groups. All the recipes in this chapter are not only new taste experiences for your baby, they start to work in vital nutrients, too.

What to give

Milk is still babies' main source of nutrition and they need 500 ml (17 fl oz) of breastmilk or formula a day. Babies' natural iron stores are beginning to run a bit low around now, though, so to give an iron boost cook up dark green vegetables such as spinach, kale and broccoli; lentils are good for iron, too. Vitamin C helps babies to absorb iron, so try combining iron-rich foods with citrus fruits (see our Lentils, Squash, Oranges + Tomatoes on page 32).

At 6 months old babies are ready to discover the creamy yumminess of certain dairy foods (such as full-fat natural yogurt or fromage frais, but not milk as a drink just yet). These provide calcium for growing bones. Dairy, and pulses such as lentils, are also a good source of first protein – they are easy on tiny tummies. A pulse- or dairy-containing meal once a day gives plenty of protein to help your baby grow. Your baby can also start exploring wheat-based foods, such as pastas and cereals.

Tips on texture

At 6 months or so, babies are able to use their tongues to move food from side to side. They still need super-smooth purées with no bits and that have the consistency of double cream or runny honey (see p.20). When babies start to show signs of rolling food around their mouths in a sort of early chewing, they're ready for slightly thicker purées made using less liquid. Adding some baby rice makes the texture thicker and grainier still.

Perfect timing

Once your little one is eating well once a day, it's probably time to try 2 meals daily instead. Try lunch then tea, or breakfast then lunch – whatever works best for your family.

How much?

Even though babies grow quickly, their tummies are still teeny tiny (about the size of a baby's clenched fist). At 6 months babies might eat 1–2 ice cubes of food at each meal. Keep things relaxed and watch out for signs that your baby is ready to stop (see p.12).

Tingling taste buds

Variety is so important! Sprinkle different spices and herbs into your baby's food for taste adventures (heat dried herbs through completely, purée the leaves of any fresh herbs and don't leave woody bits). Don't forget a rainbow of veg and those different proteins from pulses and dairy, too!

Allergy check

If you have a family history of allergies such as eczema and asthma, or of any food allergies, take care when you introduce dairy or wheat to your baby's diet (see p.21).

Water or milk?

Many of the purées in this chapter suggest diluting with boiled water, but you could use cooking liquid or your baby's usual milk, if you prefer.

Lentils, squash, oranges + tomatoes

makes **14** ice cubes   prep **10** minutes   cook **20** minutes

40 g/1½ oz dried **split red lentils**, rinsed

60 g/2¼ oz **butternut squash**, peeled, deseeded and cubed

1 **tomato**, deseeded and diced

4 tablespoons **fresh orange juice**

Place the lentils and squash in a saucepan, cover with water and bring to the boil, then reduce the heat and simmer for 10 minutes, skimming off any foam. Add the tomato and cook for a further 5 minutes until everything is tender, then drain.

Purée the lentils, squash and tomato with the orange juice in a food processor, or using a hand blender, until smooth.

Leeks, cheese + potatoes

makes **18** ice cubes   prep **10** minutes   cook **25** minutes

1 tablespoon **olive oil**

1 **leek**, trimmed and chopped

1 **potato** (about 200 g/7 oz), peeled and diced

1 teaspoon **thyme leaves**

10 g/¼ oz **mature Cheddar cheese**, finely grated

Heat the oil in a saucepan over a low heat and cook the leek for 5 minutes until softened. Add the potato and thyme, cover with water, bring to the boil, then reduce the heat and simmer for 15 minutes, or until the potato is tender. Drain, reserving the cooking water. Purée the vegetables with the cheese and 6–7 tablespoons of the cooking water in a food processor, or using a hand blender, until smooth. For a smoother purée, pass it through a sieve after blending.

Green beans + peas

makes 8 ice cubes **prep** 5 minutes **cook** 10 minutes

100 g/3½ oz **green beans**, trimmed and halved

100 g/3½ oz **frozen peas**

Steam or boil the beans in a saucepan over a medium heat for 3 minutes. Add the peas and cook for a further 2–3 minutes until the vegetables are tender.

Purée the vegetables with 100 ml/ 3½ fl oz boiled water in a food processor, or using a hand blender, until the peas are completely broken down and the mixture is smooth. For a smoother purée, pass it through a sieve after blending.

Swede + parsnips

makes 13 ice cubes **prep** 5 minutes **cook** 20 minutes

¼ **swede** (about 100 g/3½ oz), peeled and diced

1 small **parsnip** (about 75 g/ 2½ oz), peeled and diced

5 tablespoons **baby's usual milk**

Steam or boil the swede in a saucepan over a medium heat for 15 minutes. Add the parsnip and cook for a further 5 minutes until tender. Purée with the milk in a food processor, or using a hand blender, until smooth.

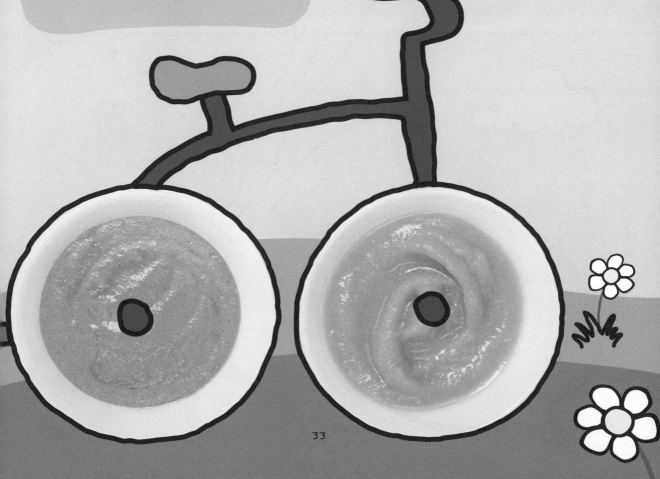

1

Sweet potatoes + red peppers

makes 17 ice cubes   **prep** 5 minutes   **cook** 15 minutes

1 **sweet potato** (about 250 g/9 oz), peeled and cubed

½ small **red pepper**, deseeded and chopped

Steam or boil the sweet potato in a saucepan over a medium heat for 5 minutes. Add the pepper and cook for 10 minutes more until the potatoes are tender and cooked through. In a food processor or using a hand blender, purée with 3–4 tablespoons boiled water until smooth.

2

Red cabbage + apples

makes 12 ice cubes   **prep** 10 minutes   **cook** 20 minutes

¼ **red cabbage** (about 70 g/2½ oz), finely chopped

2 **eating apples**, peeled, cored and cut into bite-sized pieces

Put the ingredients in a saucepan. Pour in 125 ml/4 fl oz water, cover with a lid, and bring almost to boiling point over a medium heat. Reduce the heat to low and simmer for 15–18 minutes until everything is very tender. Add a further 2–3 tablespoons boiled water, then in a food processor or using a hand blender, purée until smooth.

3

Mangoes, carrots + strawberries

makes 20 ice cubes   **prep** 10 minutes   **cook** 15 minutes

2 small **carrots** (about 120 g/4 oz), peeled and sliced

½ **mango** (about 135 g/4¾ oz), peeled, stoned and chopped

4 **strawberries**, hulled and quartered

Steam or boil the carrots in a saucepan over a medium heat for 12–15 minutes until very tender. In a food processor or using a hand blender, purée the carrots, mango and strawberries until smooth.

4

Butternut squash, sweetcorn + peas

makes 21 ice cubes   **prep** 10 minutes   **cook** 15 minutes

½ **butternut squash** (about 400 g/14 oz), peeled, deseeded and cubed

60 g/2¼ oz **frozen peas**

100 g/3½ oz no-salt and no-sugar canned **sweetcorn**, drained

Steam or boil the butternut squash in a saucepan over a medium heat for 10 minutes until almost cooked. Add the peas and sweetcorn and cook for 5 minutes more until everything is tender. In a food processor or using a hand blender, purée with 5 tablespoons boiled water until smooth.

Carrots + turnips

 makes **12** ice cubes
 prep **5** minutes
 cook **15** minutes

2 large **carrots** (about 280 g/10 oz), peeled and thinly sliced

280 g/10 oz **turnip**, peeled and diced

Steam or boil the carrots and turnip in a saucepan over a medium heat for 10–12 minutes, or until tender.

Purée the vegetables with 3 tablespoons of boiled water in a food processor, or using a hand blender, until smooth.

Swede, carrots + cinnamon

 makes **30** ice cubes
 prep **5** minutes
 cook **20** minutes

1/3 **swede** (about 175 g/6 oz), peeled and diced

2 **carrots** (about 150 g/5½ oz), peeled and thinly sliced

A generous pinch of **ground cinnamon**

Steam or boil the swede over a medium heat for 10 minutes. Add the carrots and cook for a further 10 minutes until the vegetables are tender. Purée with the cinnamon and 125 ml/4 fl oz boiled water in a food processor, or using a hand blender, until smooth.

Peas, courgettes, mint + rice

 makes **8** ice cubes
 prep **5** minutes
 cook **15** minutes

25 g/1 oz **white basmati rice**

1 **courgette** (about 150 g/5½ oz), diced

40 g/1½ oz **frozen peas**

4 **mint** leaves

Cook the rice according to the packet instructions until tender. Meanwhile, steam or boil the courgette over a medium heat for 5 minutes. Add the peas and cook for a further 3 minutes until the vegetables are tender. Purée the vegetables with the cooked rice, the mint and 2 tablespoons of boiled water, in a food processor, or using a hand blender, until the mixture is smooth. For a smoother purée, pass it through a sieve after blending.

Pears + avocado

 serves **1**
 prep **10** minutes
 cook **no cook**

½ small ripe **pear**, peeled, cored and chopped

¼ small ripe **avocado**, peeled, stoned and chopped

2 tablespoons **natural yogurt** or **baby's usual milk**, plus extra if needed

A squeeze of **lemon juice**

Purée the pear, avocado, yogurt or milk and lemon juice in a food processor, or using a hand blender, until smooth, adding a little extra milk if necessary.

Broccoli, cauliflower + courgettes

 makes **15** ice cubes
 prep **10** minutes
 cook **10** minutes

½ small head **broccoli** (about 150 g/5½ oz), cut into small florets

⅓ small head **cauliflower** (about 150 g/5½ oz), cut into small florets

1 **courgette** (about 150 g/5½ oz), diced

1 teaspoon chopped **parsley**

Steam or boil the vegetables in a saucepan over a medium heat for 7–8 minutes until tender. Add the parsley and heat through. Purée with 3–4 tablespoons of boiled water in a food processor, or using a hand blender, until smooth. For a smoother purée, pass it through a sieve after blending.

Peaches + blueberries

 makes **5** ice cubes
 prep **5** minutes
 cook **no cook**

3 ripe **peaches**, halved, stoned and diced

80 g/2¾ oz **blueberries**

Purée the peach and blueberries with 3 tablespoons of water in a food processor, or using a hand blender, until all the fruit skin is broken down and the mixture is smooth. To make the purée smoother, pass it through a sieve after blending.

oats, bananas + mixed spice

 makes **12** ice cubes
 prep **5** minutes
 cook **10** minutes

25 g/1 oz **porridge oats**

200 ml/7 fl oz **baby's usual milk**, plus extra if needed

A large pinch of **ground mixed spice**

1 small ripe **banana**, sliced

Place the oats, milk and spice in a small saucepan and bring to the boil, then reduce to a simmer for 8–10 minutes, stirring frequently, until the oats are soft. Purée with the banana in a food processor, or using a hand blender, until smooth, adding extra milk if necessary.

Sweet potatoes, carrots, cheese + broccoli

 makes **10** ice cubes
 prep **10** minutes
 cook **15** minutes

1 small **sweet potato** (about 150 g/5½ oz), peeled and diced

1 small **carrot** (about 60 g/2¼ oz), peeled and thinly sliced

¼ small head **broccoli** (about 90 g/3¼ oz), cut into small florets

10 g/¼ oz **Cheddar cheese**, finely grated

Steam or boil the sweet potato in a saucepan over a medium heat for 5 minutes. Add the carrot and cook for a further 5 minutes, then add the broccoli and continue to cook for a further 5 minutes until all the vegetables are tender. Purée the vegetables with the cheese and 4 tablespoons of boiled water in a food processor, or using a hand blender, until smooth.

Broccoli, cauliflower + courgettes

Sweet potatoes, carrots, cheese + broccoli

oats, bananas + mixed spice

Peaches + blueberries

Papaya
+ raspberries

Butter beans,
parsnips +
carrots

Chickpeas,
courgettes,
carrots +
coriander

Sweet
potatoes,
squash, apples
+ blueberries

Papaya + raspberries

makes **6** ice cubes — prep **5** minutes — cook **no cook**

1 **papaya**, peeled, deseeded and diced

70 g/2½ oz **raspberries**

Purée the papaya and raspberries in a food processor, or using a hand blender, until smooth.

Butter beans, parsnips + carrots

makes **16** ice cubes — prep **5** minutes — cook **15** minutes

1 **parsnip** (about 150 g/5½ oz), peeled and diced

2 **carrots** (about 150 g/5½ oz), peeled and thinly sliced

100 g/3½ oz canned **butter beans** in water, drained and rinsed

Steam or boil the parsnip and carrots over a medium heat for 10–12 minutes until tender. Purée with the butter beans and 6 tablespoons boiled water in a food processor, or using a hand blender, until smooth.

Chickpeas, courgettes, carrots + coriander

makes **10** ice cubes — prep **5** minutes — cook **15** minutes

1 **carrot** (about 75 g/2½ oz), peeled and thinly sliced

1 small **courgette** (about 100 g/3½ oz), diced

10 **coriander** leaves

100 g/3½ oz canned **chickpeas** in water, drained and rinsed

Steam or boil the carrot and courgette in a saucepan over a medium heat for 8–10 minutes until they are tender. Add the coriander leaves and heat through. Purée with the chickpeas and 3–4 tablespoons of boiled water in a food processor, or using a hand blender, until smooth.

Sweet potatoes, squash, apples + blueberries

makes **13** ice cubes — prep **10** minutes — cook **15** minutes

⅓ **butternut squash** (about 150 g/ 5½ oz), peeled, deseeded and diced

1 small **sweet potato** (about 150 g/ 5½ oz), peeled and diced

3 small **eating apples**, peeled, cored and diced

25 g/1 oz **blueberries**

Steam or boil the squash and sweet potato in a saucepan over a medium heat for 10 minutes. Add the fruits and cook for a further 5 minutes until tender. Purée in a food processor, or using a hand blender, until smooth.

3 ways

Three ways with no-cook purées

Sometimes it helps to have a few quick and easy, no-cook purées up your sleeve for when time is short. All of these will rustle up in minutes and will make one hungry-baby portion. And just for fun, for each baby purée we've given a grown-up or toddler variation, too. Something for everyone!

Multi-melons + bananas

What you need

75 g/2½ oz **watermelon** flesh, deseeded and diced (you may need to sieve it if it's a bit stringy)

75 g/2½ oz **gala or cantaloupe melon** flesh, diced

1 small **banana**

1 tablespoon **natural Greek yogurt** (optional)

What to do

1. Put the melon and banana into a small bowl and whiz using a hand blender until completely smooth, then stir in the yogurt, if using.

Just for older ones

Double the recipe and take out your baby's portion. Pour 100 ml/3½ fl oz fresh apple juice into the remainder and whiz again. Serve over ice with a straw for a perfect summertime smoothie.

Our friends say...

'My baby and I were so often out and about, I created an on-the-go feeding survival kit! It had bowls with clip-top lids for purée, a little cool bag with squidgy freezer packs, and plenty of spoons in case any went on the floor!'

Peaches + cucumber cream

What you need

1 ripe **peach**, peeled and stoned, or ½ small can **peach slices in juice**

2.5 cm/1 inch **cucumber**, peeled and deseeded

1 tablespoon **natural Greek yogurt**

What to do

1. Chop the peach flesh and put it in a small bowl with the cucumber.

2. Whiz using a hand blender until completely smooth.

3. Add the Greek yogurt and stir to completely combine.

Just for older ones

Double the recipe and take out your baby's portion. In the remainder, add an extra tablespoon of yogurt and spoon into a ramekin. Sprinkle with granola and serve it up for a yummy breakfast or dessert.

Tangy kiwi + avocado

What you need

1 **kiwi fruit**

½ **avocado**

Just for older ones

If you want to use up the whole of the avocado, double the recipe, then take out what your baby needs. In the remainder add a squeeze of lemon juice and a splosh of olive oil, whiz it up and drizzle it over a green salad – delicious!

What to do

1. Peel the kiwi and chop the flesh. Put the flesh in a bowl with the avocado. Whiz using a hand blender until completely smooth.

2. Pass through a sieve to remove any remaining kiwi pips, if you like (although the pips are tiny and will be fine for babies over 7 months of age). Serve immediately.

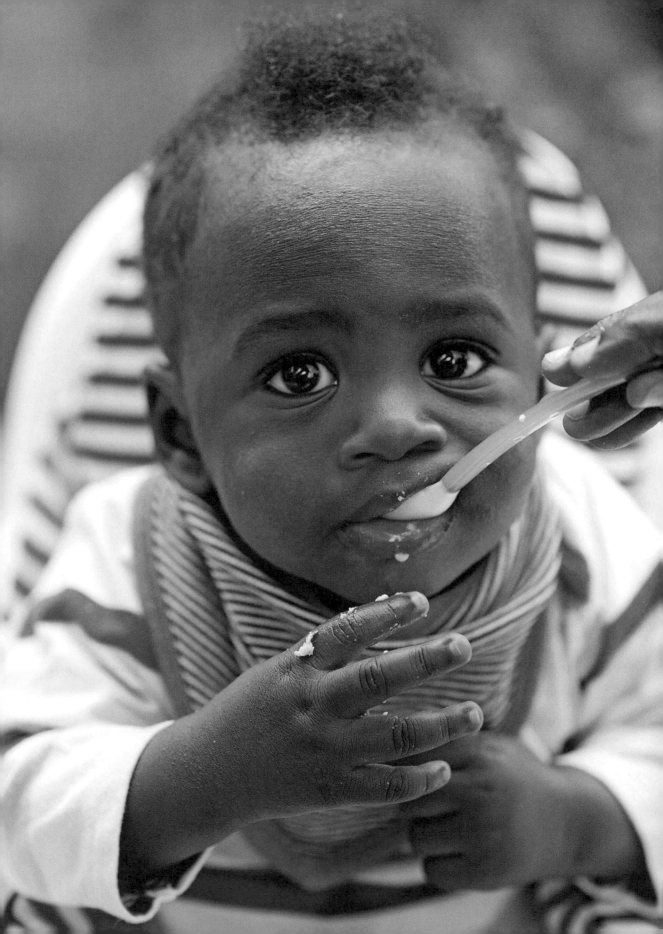

From
7 months

Your baby's digestive system is getting ready to tackle some protein foods, as well as meals with a little bit more texture. Many of the recipes in this chapter have been created as complete meals and introduce a more exciting blend of flavours and ingredients.

What to give

If you've been giving your baby a milk feed and then some purée, now is the time to start a mealtime with solids.

Continue to give 500 ml (17 fl oz) of milk a day as a drink, but your baby will also need essential nutrients, such as calcium, from food now. Introduce some meals made with milk to give calcium levels a boost for growing bones and teeth.

At 7 months your baby can start getting iron from red meat (beef and lamb), as well as pulses and all those lovely green veg. Meat, fish and pulses are also great for helping to develop immunity, as they contain iron and/or zinc.

Meat and fish (which are known as 'complete proteins') provide all the different protein building blocks your baby needs to grow. Dairy, pulses, nuts and seeds are also good protein sources, as are eggs (but cook them until both the white and yolk are solid).

Finally, babies need healthy omega-3 fats for their brain and eye development. Until now breastmilk or formula will have provided plenty, but the time has come for further supplies. Oily fish such as salmon, sardines and pilchards are all good sources.

Tips on texture

Put away the blender and use a fork or a masher instead! Go for a texture of small, soft lumps in a thicker purée. Don't worry if you think your little one doesn't have enough teeth for the job – babies are clever and quickly learn to push little soft lumps against the roof of their mouth with their tongue, to squish before they swallow.

Avoid whole peas and sweetcorn, stringy or gristly meats, and hard pasta, though, as these can pose a choking risk. You may still need to purée foods with tougher skins, such as peppers, celery, green beans, pulses and onions.

Nutritionist know-how

'Chewing not only makes food more interesting for babies, it helps to develop those little mouth muscles, encouraging speech development.'

Perfect timing

Your baby may be ready for 3 meals a day – breakfast, lunch and tea. You can give healthy snacks, but babies don't usually need them for nutrition reasons at this age (it's more about hand–eye coordination).

How much?

Depending on your little one's appetite, between 3 and 4 ice cubes of food per meal will be about the right amount. Remember to take your lead from your baby, who will tell you when enough's enough (see p.12). Of course, if you're met with tears when you take the spoon away, perhaps it's time for a bit more!

Tingling taste buds

Babies are very open-minded and experimental, so give some spices with a bit more oomph, such as cinnamon (try it with lamb; p.60) and cumin (with lentils; p.58). Introduce finger foods, too – babies love feeling more in control of their eating and these are great for testing new flavours (and for developing hand–eye coordination).

47

Little Bear's apricot porridge

makes **16** ice cubes · prep **5** minutes · cook **15** minutes

Tangy dried apricots in this warming porridge not only add a fruity twist, they also help boost your baby bear's iron stores.

What you need

40 g/1½ oz **porridge oats**

4 unsulphured, dark **dried apricots**, roughly chopped

¼ teaspoon **ground nutmeg**

300 ml/½ pint **baby's usual milk**, plus extra if needed

What to do

1. Place the oats, apricots, nutmeg and milk in a small saucepan and bring to the boil, then reduce the heat and simmer for 10 minutes, stirring frequently, or until the oats are cooked and the apricots are soft.

2. Using the back of a fork, mash the oat mixture until almost smooth, adding a little extra milk if necessary. Alternatively, purée in a food processor or using a hand blender.

You could try using a 70 g/ 2 oz pouch of Ella's Kitchen mangoes, mangoes, mangoes as a yummy alternative to the dried apricots, if you prefer.

Ella's shortcut

No-cook tuna + avocado mash

serves **2** · prep **10** minutes · cook **no cook**

Perfect for when you've no time to cook, this tasty mash can be ready in minutes.

What you need

1 **tomato**

½ small **avocado**, stoned

A squeeze of **lemon juice**

2 tablespoons drained canned **tuna chunks** in spring water

3 tablespoons drained canned **haricot beans** in water, rinsed

Baby's usual milk (optional)

What to do

1) Place the tomato in a heatproof bowl and pour enough just-boiled water over to cover. Leave for 1–2 minutes, then carefully remove with a slotted spoon and peel off the skin. Halve the tomato, scoop out and discard the seeds, then finely chop the flesh.

2) Scoop out the avocado flesh into a bowl, squeeze over a little lemon juice and add the tomato, tuna and beans. Purée using a hand blender until almost smooth, adding a little milk if necessary.

Rough + smooth

Feed the senses

A whole avocado is brilliant for teaching opposites. Let your baby feel the bumpy skin – like a crocodile! Open it up for little fingers to poke the super-smooth flesh. Talk about the textures – rough and smooth all in one!

1

Tropical pineapple zing

makes **18** ice cubes | prep **10** minutes | cook **15** minutes

What you need

25 g/1 oz **white basmati rice**

100 g/3½ oz **cottage cheese**

100 g/3½ oz **pineapple**, peeled, cored and very finely chopped

50 ml/2 fl oz **baby's usual milk**

What to do

1. Cook the rice in a small saucepan of boiling water according to the packet instructions until tender. Drain, then tip into a bowl.

2. Add the cottage cheese, pineapple and milk, then using the back of a fork, mash together until almost smooth. Alternatively, purée in a food processor or using a hand blender.

2

Cool summer soup

makes **21** ice cubes | prep **15** minutes | cook **5** minutes

What you need

1 slice of **half-white, half-wholemeal bread**, crusts removed

6 tablespoons **baby's usual milk**, plus extra if needed

3 **tomatoes**

½ **red pepper**, cored, deseeded and cut into chunks

8 cm/3¼ inch piece of **cucumber**, peeled, deseeded and roughly chopped

150 g/5½ oz canned **butter beans** in water, drained and rinsed

A squeeze of **lemon juice**

A handful of **basil** leaves

What to do

1. Place the bread in a shallow bowl, pour over the milk and leave to stand.

2. Meanwhile, steam or boil the whole tomatoes and red pepper in a saucepan over a medium heat for 3 minutes until softened. When cool enough to handle, peel off the tomato skins and discard, then halve the tomatoes and remove the seeds.

3. Tear the bread into pieces, then purée with the tomatoes, red pepper, cucumber, butter beans, lemon juice and basil in a food processor, or using a hand blender, until almost smooth, adding extra milk or boiled water if necessary.

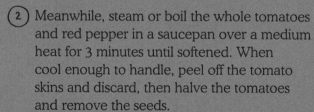
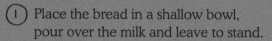

Supergreens cheese + chive pasta

 makes **18** ice cubes

 prep **5** minutes

 cook **10** minutes

What you need

50 g/1¾ oz dried **orzo** or other dried **pasta**

3 **broccoli** florets, cut into pieces

25 g/1 oz **frozen petits pois**

½ teaspoon snipped **chives**

1 tablespoon **cream cheese**

5 tablespoons **baby's usual milk**

What to do

1. Cook the pasta in a saucepan of boiling water for 3 minutes, then add the broccoli and petits pois and cook for a further 4–5 minutes, or until everything is tender. Drain, reserving the cooking water.

2. Return the pasta, vegetables and 2 tablespoons of the reserved cooking water to the pan. Add the chives, cream cheese and milk and stir together.

3. Using the back of a fork, mash the pasta mixture until almost smooth. Alternatively, purée in a food processor or using a hand blender. To make the purée smoother, pass it through a sieve after blending.

Roasty-red pesto chicken

makes **18** ice cubes · prep **15** minutes · cook **40** minutes

The juiciness of roast chicken gives a workout for little gums that are just learning to chew, and punchy pesto tingles tiny taste buds.

What you need

1 small **potato** (about 115 g/ 4 oz), peeled and thinly sliced into rounds

5 cm/2 inch piece of **leek**, white only, very thinly sliced

1 **tomato**, sliced into rounds

½ teaspoon **dried oregano**

1 teaspoon **olive oil**

1 teaspoon **red pesto** (see box, below)

1 skinless **chicken breast** (about 125 g/4½ oz)

Baby's usual milk (optional)

What to do

1. Preheat the oven to 200°C/400°F/Gas Mark 6. Place a large sheet of aluminium foil in a baking dish and arrange the potato in the middle in an even layer. Top with the leek and tomato, then sprinkle over the oregano and oil. Spoon the pesto over the chicken, then place on top of the tomato.

2. Gather up the edges of the foil and seal to make a parcel. Bake for 35–40 minutes until the potato is tender and the chicken is cooked through. Carefully open the parcel, remove the chicken and chop into four.

3. Whiz the remaining contents of the parcel with the chicken in a food processor, or using a hand blender, until finely chopped, adding a little milk if necessary.

Perfect pesto

Homemade red pesto is super-easy! Heat 1 tablespoon of extra virgin olive oil in a nonstick frying pan, fry 2 chopped cloves of garlic and 100 g/3½ oz pine nuts for 2–3 minutes. Blitz 50 g/1¾ oz basil and 6 sun-dried tomatoes (drained and patted dry) in a food processor, then add the garlic mixture, 4 tablespoons of extra virgin olive oil, 50 g/1¾ oz Parmesan cheese and 100 ml/3½ fl oz water. Blitz again. (If you leave out the sun-dried tomato, the pesto is green!) Heat through before serving.

Tasty tomato-y fish + rice

makes **24** ice cubes prep **10** minutes cook **20** minutes

Tomatoes and green beans are full of vitamin C, which helps support little immune systems. This is a quick and easy dish – increase the quantities to feed the whole family, if you like.

What you need

25 g/1 oz **white basmati rice**

3 tablespoons drained canned **haricot beans** in water, rinsed

2 **green beans**, trimmed and chopped

2 teaspoons **olive oil**

115 g/4 oz skinless, boneless **white fish fillet**, such as haddock

175 ml/6 fl oz **passata** (sieved tomatoes)

½ teaspoon **dried oregano**

What to do

1. Cook the rice in a small saucepan of boiling water according to the packet instructions until tender, adding the haricot and green beans 8 minutes before the end of the cooking time.

2. Meanwhile, heat the oil in a nonstick frying pan over a medium heat and cook the fish for 10 minutes, turning once, until cooked through. Remove the fish with a spatula and flake into bite-sized pieces, taking care to remove any bones.

3. Drain the rice and beans, then place in a pan with the fish, passata and oregano. Cook over a low heat for 5 minutes, stirring frequently, until warmed through.

4. Using the back of a fork, mash the fish mixture until almost smooth, adding a little boiled water if necessary. Alternatively, purée in a food processor or using a hand blender.

feed the senses

Super-shaker

Pop some uncooked rice in a clean plastic bottle and secure the lid. While you're rustling up this tasty dish, give the shaker to your baby to make some music for you to cook along to. Don't forget to dance! Lentils, crisped rice, and water are good shaker-fillers, too.

All aboard!

My first fish curry

makes
18
ice cubes

prep
15
minutes

cook
20
minutes

Fish is a *reeeally* healthy source of protein to help your little taste explorer grow, and the exotic flavours in this dish make it perfect for baby's first curry night.

What you need

115 g/4 oz skinless, boneless **white fish fillet**, such as haddock

150 ml/¼ pint **baby's usual milk**, plus extra if needed

1 **lemongrass stalk** (optional)

25 g/1 oz **white basmati rice**

2 **broccoli** florets

1 teaspoon **mild curry powder**

2 tablespoons **coconut milk**

What to do

1. Place the fish in a small saucepan, cover with the milk and add the lemongrass (if using). Poach the fish over a medium–low heat for 12 minutes, or until cooked through. Reserving the milk, discard the lemongrass (if used) and lift out the fish with a spatula. Flake the fish into bite-sized pieces, taking care to remove any bones.

2. Meanwhile, cook the rice in a small saucepan of boiling water according to the packet instructions until tender. In a separate saucepan, steam or boil the broccoli over a medium heat for 6–8 minutes until tender. Remove and finely chop the florets, discarding the stalks.

3. Return the fish to the pan with the reserved milk. Drain the rice and add to the fish with the broccoli, curry powder and coconut milk. Stir over a low heat until combined and warmed through.

4. Using the back of a fork, mash the fish mixture until almost smooth, adding a little extra milk if necessary. Alternatively, purée in a food processor or using a hand blender.

Full of beans pork + peppers

The combination of soft pork and cannellini beans in this recipe is fantastic for introducing a bit of texture to little gums. Spinach and pepper contain vitamin C, which helps little ones release energy to keep them full of beans, too!

What you need

1 tablespoon **olive oil**

100 g/3½ oz lean **minced pork**

1 small **onion**, finely chopped

½ small **red pepper**, cored, deseeded and diced

1 **garlic** clove, crushed

1 teaspoon **dried thyme**

300 ml/½ pint **passata** (sieved tomatoes)

2 teaspoons **tomato purée**

2 **cloves**

100 g/3½ oz canned **cannellini beans** in water, drained and rinsed

25 g/1 oz **baby spinach leaves**, stalks removed and leaves shredded

What to do

1. Heat the oil in a saucepan over a medium heat and cook the mince for 5 minutes, breaking it up with the back of a fork, until browned all over. Remove with a slotted spoon and set aside.

2. Reduce the heat slightly, add the onion to the pan and cook for 5 minutes until softened, then stir in the red pepper, garlic and thyme and cook for a further 2 minutes, stirring frequently. Return the mince to the pan.

3. Stir in the passata, tomato purée, cloves, beans, spinach and 50 ml/2 fl oz water. Bring to the boil, then reduce the heat, part-cover with a lid and simmer for 20 minutes, stirring occasionally, until the mince is cooked through. Remove the cloves.

4. Using the back of a fork, mash the mince mixture until almost smooth, adding a little boiled water if necessary. Alternatively, purée in a food processor or using a hand blender.

Sun-bleached splodges

We love a bit of mess at mealtimes, but how do you get the tomato-y blobs out of your little one's bib? We know! Pop it on a windowsill in the sunshine and the sun will bleach out the stains. Brilliant!

Very, very tasty veggie bake with lentils

makes **26** ice cubes prep **10** minutes cook **25** minutes

This dish is not only very, very tasty, it's very, very easy to make, too! It's crammed with veggies, and the cumin adds a smoky flavour for your little one to try.

What you need

1 small **sweet potato** (about 150 g/5¼ oz), peeled and cut into large bite-sized pieces

1 small **carrot** (about 60 g/2¼ oz), peeled and sliced

½ small **onion**, finely chopped

25 g/1 oz dried **split red lentils**, rinsed

150 ml/¼ pint canned **chopped tomatoes**

½ teaspoon **ground cumin**

2 hard-boiled **eggs**, yolks only, mashed

What to do

1. Place the sweet potato, carrot, onion and lentils in a saucepan, cover with water and bring to the boil. Reduce the heat, part-cover with a lid, and simmer for 15 minutes until tender, skimming off any foam that rises to the surface. Drain, reserving the cooking water.

2. Return the vegetables and lentils to the pan, add the tomatoes and cumin and stir in 2 tablespoons of the reserved cooking water. Simmer over a low heat for 5 minutes, then add the mashed egg yolks.

3. Using the back of a fork, mash the vegetable mixture until almost smooth, adding a little extra reserved cooking water if necessary. Alternatively, purée in a food processor or using a hand blender.

Ella's shortcut

Try using 2 x 70 g/2 oz pouches of Ella's Kitchen sweet potatoes, sweet potatoes in place of the sweet potato itself, and save on the chopping time!

Sweet + spicy lamb + date couscous

makes **18** ice cubes · prep **10** minutes · cook **40** minutes

Delight tiny taste buds with this delicious combination of exciting new flavours. The dates give a little burst of sweetness, while the cinnamon adds warming spice.

What you need

1 teaspoon **olive oil**

100 g/3½ oz **minced lamb**

1 small **garlic** clove, crushed

1 **carrot** (about 75 g/2½ oz), peeled and finely chopped

2 **pitted dried dates**, chopped

150 ml/¼ pint **passata** (sieved tomatoes)

½ teaspoon **ground cinnamon**

15 g/½ oz **couscous**

What to do

1) Heat the oil in a saucepan over a medium heat and cook the lamb mince for 5 minutes, breaking it up with the back of a fork, until browned all over.

2) Stir in the garlic, then add the carrot, dates, passata and cinnamon and bring almost to the boil. Reduce the heat, part-cover with a lid and simmer for 25 minutes until the sauce has reduced and thickened.

3) Meanwhile, place the couscous in a heatproof bowl and pour over enough just-boiled water to cover. Stir, cover with a plate and leave for 5 minutes until tender. Drain if necessary and add to the pan with the lamb. Cook for a further 5 minutes until tender, adding a splash of water if necessary.

4) Using the back of a fork, mash the lamb mixture until almost smooth, adding a little boiled water if necessary. Alternatively, purée in a food processor or using a hand blender.

Keep smiling!

Smiley mealtimes keep babies happy about food. If your baby doesn't feel like eating, even if it's something *deeelicious*, that's okay. Don't look sad. Babies have hungry days and less hungry days – just like we do!

Wrapped + roasted salmon + beans

 makes **18** ice cubes

 prep **15** minutes

 cook **35** minutes

Baking salmon in a little parcel keeps all the juiciness locked in, which means the salmon flakes will be super-soft for your baby's gums. Ground coriander adds a tasty twist.

What you need

1 small **potato** (about 115 g/4 oz), peeled and diced

115 g/4 oz skinless, boneless **salmon fillet**

½ teaspoon **ground coriander**

15 g/½ oz **unsalted butter**, cubed

2 **green beans**, trimmed and thinly sliced

5 tablespoons **baby's usual milk**, plus extra if needed

What to do

1. Preheat the oven to 190°C/375°F/Gas Mark 5. Place a large sheet of aluminium foil in a baking dish and arrange the potatoes in the middle in an even layer. Add 1 tablespoon of water, then top with the salmon. Sprinkle over the coriander and dot with the butter.

2. Gather up the edges of the foil and seal to make a parcel. Bake in the oven for 30 minutes until the fish and potato are cooked through.

3. Meanwhile, steam or boil the beans in a saucepan over a medium heat for 5 minutes until tender. Drain if necessary, then finely chop and return to the pan.

4. Open the foil parcel, tip the contents into the pan with the beans and add the milk. Heat through gently. Using the back of a fork, mash together until almost smooth, adding a little extra milk if necessary. Alternatively, purée in a food processor or using a hand blender.

Our friends say...

'When I was breastfeeding, I ate lots of different spices so my little one got used to strong flavours in her milk feeds. It seemed to work – she's showing signs of becoming a really adventurous eater!'

3
ways

Three ways with Ella's Kitchen Friends

We think the best weaning advice of all is passed on by word of mouth – from mums, dads, grannies and granddads, aunts and uncles, and from one friend to another. Some of those nuggets of wisdom might strike a chord and fire up an idea, and others might reassure, or make you smile and know that you aren't alone.

We've asked some of our Ella's Kitchen Friends for the best pieces of weaning advice others had given them. These are the ones we especially hope will inspire you to relax and enjoy this special time with your baby.

Take a look at our Weaning Adventure map at the end of the book. This fun guide is designed to help you and your little one on your weaning journey.

Stick up lists

When I started weaning my little girl, the best piece of advice I think anyone ever gave me was to stick up a step-by-step list of when to introduce certain foods. It was a simple idea, but it made a big difference to us. It simplified the weaning process, which initially felt quite daunting. Once it was up, that list meant I could look on the fridge and plan my shopping with my baby in mind, knowing everything I bought for her was safe and providing the right nutrients. It also made it exciting when it was time to introduce something new – we'd celebrate with lots of smiles and cries of 'Well done!' Everyone was happy!

Saffron, mum to Allana (age 3) and Iris (age 8 months)

Look at a week

I used to think my little one was such a fussy eater and that he wasn't eating enough. Then, my health visitor told me I shouldn't think of his diet as something that happens over a day, but over the course of a week, or even a month. That was my lightbulb moment!

It sounds a bit grown-up, but I kept a food diary of everything he ate and the amount of time he spent breastfeeding every day for a month. It was amazing to see that some days he ate precious little in the way of food, but he certainly made up for it on others! Seeing everything written down made me realize that over a whole week, and then a whole month, he was eating perfectly well and getting everything he needed – he was just doing it his own special way!

Angie, mum to Reece (age 5) and Summer (age 2)

Turn the table

My baby boy was absolutely brilliant at eating in his high chair in the early days, but when he got a bit more mobile, he started objecting to sitting at the table. He wanted to eat on the move all the time!

My dad told me not to let it become a battle (eventually he'd sit where the rest of us were sitting), and to think of 'creative' tables around our home. At teatime, I took to laying out a picnic rug on the kitchen floor, with a few teddies, too; on warm days, we'd picnic in the garden. Teatimes were so much more relaxed this way that eventually, after only a couple of weeks and without him even really noticing, he was back in his high chair and eating at the table happily. Occasionally – even though he's now 3 – we still have an indoor picnic… just for fun!

Sophie, mum to Tristan (age 3) and Alice (age 10 months)

The tiny tastebud journey!

This adventure map is here to help you + your little one on your weaning journey. Follow the path at a pace that suits your baby – every baby is different so don't worry if some steps take a little longer. The most important thing is to have fun on your journey together to the big table!

Very first tastes
First 2 weeks

Start here!

Veggie tastes and baby's milk are all your baby needs for now. Tiny tummies can't have:
• Dairy + eggs • Grains + pulses • Poultry + meat • Fish + shellfish • Nuts + seeds • Gluten, wheat, mustard, celeriac, celery, honey

Weaning wisdom
• 500–600 ml (17 fl oz– 1 pint) baby's usual milk per day
• Super-smooth puree, texture like runny honey
• 2–3 teaspoons, once a day

Week 1
Start with veggies, one taste at a time:
Potatoes • Broccoli • Cauliflower • Green beans • Cabbages • Avocado • Peas

Week 2
More veggie purees, one by one:
Courgettes • Brussels sprouts • Aubergine • Carrots • Parsnips • Butternut squash • Swede

6+ months

Weaning wisdom
• 500 ml (17 fl oz) baby's usual milk per day; tap water
• Smooth texture, but slightly thicker
• 1–2 ice cubes, twice a day

Veggies + fruit
All veg + fruit are great, and in puree combos, too

Dairy + eggs
Try purees with:
Natural full-fat yoghurt, fromage frais or crème fraiche • Full-fat cow's milk • Pasteurized cheese • Well-cooked eggs

Grains + pulses
Try purees with:
Cereal foods (such as pasta) • Rice • Lentils • Chickpeas • Beans, including soya beans

7+ months

Weaning wisdom
• 500 ml (17 fl oz) baby's usual milk per day; tap water; well-diluted fresh juice
• Mashed-up, very soft texture with very small, soft lumps
• 3–4 ice cubes, 3 times a day

Dairy + eggs
Now your baby can try mashed-up meals with yummy cheese

other yummy foods
Now your baby can try a little yummy honey

Poultry + meat
Try mashed-up meals with:
Soft, lean poultry • Soft, lean meat

Fish + shellfish
Try mashed-up meals with:
Salmon + white fish • Canned tuna • Sardines + mackerel (limit oily fish to twice a week) • Well-cooked prawns

10+ months

Nuts + seeds
Try mashed-up meals with:
Smooth peanut butter • Finely ground nuts • Finely ground seeds

Weaning wisdom
• As 7+ months
• Soft pea-sized lumps + chunks in a thick puree
• Heaped bowl 3 times a day + 2 snacks

12+ months

Nuts + seeds
Try chunkier meals with:
Finely chopped nuts • Finely chopped seeds

other yummy foods
Tingle tiny tastebuds with stronger spices, such as ginger

Weaning wisdom
• 500 ml (17 fl oz) full-fat cow's milk daily; tap water + juice as 7+ months
• Baby bite-sized pieces
• Heaped bowl 3 times a day + 2 snacks

Dairy + eggs
Try meals made with:
Well-cooked unpasteurized soft or blue cheese • Runny eggs

one last thing...
Even though your baby can eat anything now, some foods still pose a choking risk:
Whole nuts • Whole grapes + other whole fruits with shiny skins
Finally, always avoid adding sugar or salt to your little one's meals.

Hooray!
Your little one has made it to the big table! Big thumbs up!